*The Boy Airman:
An Absolute Stranger
to Fear*

A Tribute to
Hugh Mortimer Petty
Surgeon
1898-1975

The Boy Airman:
An Absolute Stranger
to Fear

Richard Petty

Pen & Sword
AVIATION

First published in 2014 by Richard Petty, London W1

and reprinted in this format in 2015 by
PEN & SWORD AVIATION
An imprint of
Pen & Sword Books Ltd
47 Church Street, Barnsley
South Yorkshire
S70 2AS

ISBN 978 1 47384 905 1

A CIP catalogue record for this book is
available from the British Library

Typeset by Dinah Drazin

Printed and bound in England
By CPI Group (UK) Ltd, Croydon, CR0 4YY

Pen & Sword Books Ltd incorporates the Imprints of Pen & Sword Aviation,
Pen & Sword Family History, Pen & Sword Maritime, Pen & Sword Military,
Pen & Sword Discovery, Pen & Sword Politics, Pen & Sword Atlas,
Pen & Sword Archaeology, Wharncliffe Local History, Leo Cooper,
Wharncliffe True Crime, Wharncliffe Transport, Pen & Sword Select,
Pen & Sword Military Classics, The Praetorian Press, Claymore Press,
Remember When, Seaforth Publishing and Frontline Publishing

For a complete list of Pen & Sword titles please contact
PEN & SWORD BOOKS LIMITED
47 Church Street, Barnsley, South Yorkshire, S70 2AS, England
E-mail: enquiries@pen-and-sword.co.uk
Website: www.pen-and-sword.co.uk

The 'boy airman' is the most wonderful of all the wonderful combatants in this war. Those in authority like to catch him young, for his 'nerve' is better and he comes into training as an absolute stranger to fear.

– George Brown Burgin, The Idler, c. 1918

This book is published to coincide with the exhibition
'The Boy Airman' at Harrow School
May to December 2014.

Acknowledgements

The distinguished curator of the Old Speech Room Gallery, Julia Walton, is the inspiration behind the resuscitation of my father's snapshots of his teenage years as a naval pilot towards the end of the First World War. There are many professional photographs of this horrific period, but we think it is unusual to be able to associate intimate images with a personal narrative.

Robin Bell, one of the world's finest black and white printers, is responsible for the reproduction of the tiny thumb nails and ancient negatives – without any digital aid. My grateful thanks to him for a truly heroic effort.

Many thanks also to Azadeh Fatehrad. She has worked assiduously to create a high resolution archive of all my father's images.

Dr Lucy Scholes has been vital to all other practical matters from typing the text to co-ordinating the design elements of this book. Thank you so much Lucy.

Foreword

'The Great War' drained Britain's vital pool of talent, intellect and muscle. A third of virile males, two and a half million, were dead or disabled.

The material cost of this idiot conflict is unknowable. The colossal British National Debt was funded by profits of old empire and new American dollars.

"Eventually, the United States became the larder, arsenal and bank of the Allies and acquired a direct interest in Allied victory..."

By 1918, the Empires of Germany, Austro-Hungary and Turkey were bankrupt or defunct: the decimation of ancient hierarchies destabilised European society, and rule by exclusive coterie was severely weakened.

Tides of gold had ebbed and flowed; industry and science had been urgently invigorated.

Hence, political opportunism became viable, and further conflicts of interest inevitable.

My father served in both 'World Wars', just 21 years apart – his life made flotsam by unpredictable events called history.

Richard Petty
April 2014

Waiting to enlist outside the Central London Recruiting Depot.

I

War, Germany, Act.
– The War Telegram, 4th August 1914

To make war on Germany started as a truly popular, even populist, concept.

Swarms of enthusiastic young men swamped recruitment offices, lemming-like, shoulder to shoulder, in dense cheering crowds, desperately anxious to fight for King and Country – to the very death: "God save the King, long live the King."

By the end of September, 750,000 had enlisted, goaded by the humiliating retreat of the British Expeditionary Force at the Battle of Mons, the revelatory first contact with the swarming armies of the Hun.

This was not a religious or ideological war: it was not a war between belligerent dynasties. No clear explanations were on offer: perhaps a militaristic but weak German Kaiser manipulated by overweeningly ambitious Prussian generals? Perhaps the ineptitude of elderly plutocratic Liberal politicians distracted by a mutinous Ireland? One too many intricate treaties, the infamous 'scraps of paper'? France still rancorous after a century of defeat, dishonour and disorder?

Certainly not fortuitous pot shots by a disaffected teenage Serbian student in Sarajevo.

Further to confound any reasonable rationale, Britain's royal

Arrest of Gavrilo Princip, age 24, one of nine children of a Serbian postman, the assassin of Archduke Franz Ferdinand, the heir to the Austro-Hungarian Empire, in Sarajevo, 28th June 1914.

His Majesty King George V, Emperor of India,
Defender of the Faith.

Seine Majestät Kaiser Wilhelm II, Deutscher Kaiser
und König von Preussen.

HMS *Dreadnought*, 1907.

Louis Blériot in flight, 1909.

family had been Hanoverian – German – since 1714, since King George I, who spoke no English.

More recently, Queen Victoria had married her first cousin, the love of her life, Prince Albert of Saxe-Coburg and Gotha, 'Albert the Good', the dedicated protagonist of Great Britain and its Empire.

The current head of state was King George V, disciplinarian parent and distinguished philatelist, scion of the same blood, King and Emperor, Defender of the Faith.

Kaiser Wilhelm II, 'Kaiser Bill', the son of the self-appointed German Emperor, and King of Prussia, was Queen Victoria's first grandson, diminutive and palsied, loathing his English mother, bristling with self-glory and bombast – intensely jealous of Britain's empire.

But it was perfectly evident that the man on the street, the hoi polloi, was up for a scrap whatever the reason. This was going to be a people's war – everybody's war.

"We have won every other war, haven't we? – Why not this one?"

Britain's last major conflict had ended in 1815. The Napoleonic Wars had been conducted with manoeuvre, musketry, cannon, cavalry and sailing ship. This new war was to be fought, rat-like, in troglodyte trenches and tunnels – with high explosive, poison gas and machine gun – latterly with the tank.

Further novel dimensions were added to the industrialised armamentarium.

The sailing ships, Nelson's 'wooden walls', metamorphosed through 'iron-clads' into monstrous 'dreadnoughts', heavily armoured battleships carrying awesome fire power in rotating turrets.

The Wright brothers launched their 'flyer' successfully in

1903. Blériot 'flew' the 22 miles of the English Channel in 1909. Alcock and Brown crossed the Atlantic non-stop in 1919. Between times, the canvas and wood 'kite' – the 'aeroplane' – developed into a sophisticated weapon carrying machine guns, bombs and cameras.

'Flying machines' fast became a serious nuisance, and attracted substantial private investment – and 'daring young men'.

2

To Germany –
You are blind like us. Your hurt no man designed,
And no man claimed the conquest of your land.
                    – Charles Hamilton Sorley, killed aged 20, 1915

It is a sin to believe evil of others, but it is seldom a mistake.
                    – H. L. Mencken, *A Little Book in C Major*, 1916

The short cut from Germany to France was through Belgium.

The unheralded invasion of Belgium accommodated the massive outflanking right hook of the covert Schlieffen Plan; it was essential to the quick capture of Paris and the subjugation of France.

To dominate all Europe was the objective of the All-Highest, *der Allerhöchster*, the Kaiser, to impose the rule of the *Übermenschen*, and the *Kultur* of his superior German nation – 'the desperate delusion' of Hegel and Nietzsche.

The self-absorbed and irresolute British government had failed to anticipate the well-timed German strike, but the press propagandists reacted promptly to the outrageous violation of a neutral state.

Initially the Belgian Army had offered some stubborn defence, but this was soon overwhelmed. With ruthless and ferocious efficiency, the Germans suppressed any civilian complaint, initiating a reign of terror throughout the tiny country.

Belgium was typically depicted as a shackled, bound and gagged lissome beauty about to be sullied at pistol point by a jack-booted, leering, obese Hun.

If the British public by now had any remaining doubts as to the purpose of this war, they were swept aside by an astonishingly ill-conceived act of callous violence.

Nurse Edith Cavell was executed by a German Army firing squad.

She had been the English Matron of the Red Cross Hospital in Brussels.

At her summary court martial, she had not deigned to answer the charge of helping Allied soldiers to escape to the neutral Netherlands.

The pervasive image of the filthy, pitiless, despicable Hun was given sharp and vivid focus – the epitome of a vile enemy, to be curbed and crushed without hesitation.

King George V changed his family name from Saxe-Coburg and Gotha to Windsor.

Furious public reaction to the murder of our nurse gave further urgent impetus to recruitment. Lord Kitchener was assembling his volunteer army, 'Kitchener's Mob', and he had a voracious appetite for fit young men.

He was fully aware that the professional army, the heavily outnumbered British Expeditionary Force – the 70,000 'Old Contemptibles'[1] – was melting away at an alarming rate in vitally delaying the Huns' advance on Paris.

To enlist and fight overseas, law dictated that volunteers had to be nineteen years old or more. However, recruiting officers

1. The Kaiser had purportedly ordered his armies, numbering some two million men-at-arms, to sweep away the 'contemptible' little British army.

A Fact, indictment of German soldier's murder of boy, Maastricht, Belgium, 1915, Louis Raemaeker.

The Seduction, German rape of Belgium, 1915, Louis Raemaeker.

Edith Cavell.

Death of Edith Cavell, 1915, Louis Raemaeker.

Field Marshal Horatio Herbert Kitchener,
First Earl Kitchener of Khartoum.

Boy (1st class) John Travers Cornwell of HMS *Chester*, age 16 at the
Battle of Jutland, 31st May, 1916, posthumous VC.

did not require proof of age or identity, and boys lied.

Boys thereafter made up a significant proportion of all the Services.

On the first day of the Battle of the Somme in 1916, 500 boy soldiers were killed or wounded. By the end of the battle, 18,000 were dead or maimed: the youngest was 14. By the end of the war an estimated 250,000 had been recruited.

There was considerable public consternation about the use of underage soldiers, which was given a voice in parliament by Sir Arthur Markham, Liberal MP for Mansfield. He was castigated by many as being anti-war, and there were sharp divisions within the House of Commons.

In a challenging statement to the House, he said, "There has been fraud, deceit and lying practised by the War Office."

Markham was opposed by Harold Tennant, the Under-Secretary of State for War. Tennant returned that the War Office was the victim of deceit in as much as it was the boys who had lied about their age.

As a result of Markham's persistence, the War Office directed the Army in France to return all boy soldiers to Britain. The onus was given to senior army officers to effect this. Needless to relate, there was no great enthusiasm to lose trained soldiers, and there was no significant response.

Markham died in August 1916, aged 50. His legacy, however, was embedded in the 1916 Military Service Act, which specified that "Men from 18 to 41 years old were liable to be called up for service in the Army unless they were married, widowed with children, serving in the Royal Navy, a minister of religion, or working in one of a number of reserved occupations".

Thereafter all conscripts were obliged to provide evidence of age and identity.

3

Wouldst thou learn the secret of the sea?
Only those who brave its dangers comprehend its mystery.
– Henry Wadsworth Longfellow, 1850

By 1915, more than two million British and Imperial soldiers were engaged on the 'Western Front', in France and Flanders, fighting 'Fritz' eyeball to bloody eyeball, across the no-man's land of trenches stretching from the Belgian beaches to the border with Switzerland – 450 miles.

For command of the sea, the arms race between Britain and Germany in the early 1900s resulted in the creation of fleets of increasingly powerful battleships and multitudes of attendant cruisers and destroyers.

The price of these Leviathans was enormous – around £2.4 million each – at today's value, £888 million.

In 2014 the new Astute Class state of the art hunter-killer submarines will cost more than £1 billion each: we might be able to afford seven.

In 1914 Britain sailed 36 modern battleships, 12 battlecruisers, around 60 armoured cruisers and hundreds of supporting light cruisers and destroyers.

Purportedly these ships would defend our intercontinental trade routes. This same argument was used by the Germans in the early and fruitless negotiations surrounding relative sea power.

By 1914, after gargantuan effort and expenditure, and political blood-letting, Britain had superseded the German production of capital ships by two to one.

Fear of invasion of our island has always been, of course, our national paranoia. The two Napoleons had contemplated the temptation intermittently over the previous hundred years. The tiny Channel Island of Alderney had been massively fortified in the 1850s, its harbour constructed to succour the Home Fleet, subduing any aggressive aspirations of the French Navy locked up, yet again, in Cherbourg.

The French threat was finally put to rest through the *Entente Cordiale* of 1904. Our distrait Liberal government had concluded, somewhat tardily and reluctantly, that the potential invader might now be Germany.

The personality behind the modernisation of the Royal Navy was the formidable Lord Fisher, 'Jacky' Fisher, Admiral of the Fleet; First Sea Lord again, aged 73 on the outbreak of war. His stellar career, having started in wooden square riggers, had enabled him to persuade ever parsimonious politicians to invest in torpedoes, destroyers, the first dreadnoughts, turbine engines, oil fuel instead of coal, daily bread baked aboard ship rather than weevil infested biscuit, and, above all, the fast and furious battlecruiser – the 'Splendid Cat': he was a naval hero to rival Nelson.

His German counterpart was Grand Admiral Alfred von Tirpitz, Secretary of State of the Imperial Naval Office. In his quest for European dominance, the preposterous Kaiser had commanded the poor benighted von Tirpitz to expand the diminutive Prussian Coastal Defence Force, to create an Imperial Fleet capable of challenging British sea power.

Perfectly obviously this was a serious non-starter. Von Tirpitz,

Admiral of the Fleet John Arbuthnot 'Jacky' Fisher, First Baron
Fisher, born in Ceylon, eldest of eleven children to Captain William
Fisher of 78th Highlanders (Seaforth and Camerons, Queen's own
Highlanders).

Grand Admiral Alfred von Tirpitz.

'U-boats' – *die Unterseebotte.*

being no fool, redirected as much investment as was politically expedient into the development of the novel 'submarine'. The inherent invisibility of this phantasmal weapon, armed with the British invention of an effective torpedo, had given rise to a highly attractive concept.

It was perfectly possible, he thought, that, given adequate numbers, a German submarine fleet could sink a critical proportion of British capital war ships and maritime traders, sufficient as to lay bare our island fastness to famine and, indeed, invasion.

Von Tirpitz had certainly had a seminal notion.

The nuclear powered, nuclear armed submarine is now every aspirant super-power's global bludgeon.

4

*... miles of warships running at high speed and in absolute black-
ness through the narrow Straits, bearing with them into the broad
waters of the North the safeguard of considerable affairs ... the King's
ships were at sea.*

– Winston Churchill, 1923

The British Grand Fleet assembled at their war stations; Scapa
Flow, its headquarters, in the Orkney Islands, the greatest
of natural harbours, and the Firth of Forth, giving sheltered
anchorage and access to the naval dockyards of Rosyth.

From these northernmost outposts of Britain, the Grand
Fleet could blockade Germany, entrapping the nascent German Imperial High Seas Fleet in their harbours of Kiel and
Wilhelmshaven, importantly denying any aspirational infesta-
tion of Atlantic trade routes.

The battle ground was the North Sea, 600 miles long and
360 miles wide, an arena of 290,000 square miles; Scotland and
England to the west, and to the east, the coast of Europe from
Norway and Denmark to France.

It was this vast cockpit of water that the Grand Fleet was
required to patrol, and to attempt to catch its inferior foe, the
German High Seas Fleet, in the open – unprotected by its
minefields – and annihilate it.

*   *   *

Scapa Flow, *Orkney*, 1917, Sir John Lavery.

The British Grand Fleet at anchor in the Firth of Forth.

The North Sea

A significant number of codebooks had been captured from German ships and spies from as far afield as Russia and Australia.

With these keys, 'Room 40' of the Admiralty could decipher, albeit slowly, the enemy's diplomatic and military signalling. Room 40 was under the superlative management of a previous Director of Naval Education, Sir James Alfred Ewing, seen as the archetypal Sherlock Holmes, a talented physicist and engineer, a Scot and an obsessive cryptographic hobbyist.

The first cryptic 'word-cross' puzzle had been invented by the Liverpudlian journalist Arthur Wynne; it had been published in the *New York World* on 21st December 1913.

Julius Caesar's substitution cipher is a simple alphabetical offset algorithm; the key is the number of characters to offset it. If the key number is 3, the first letter of the alphabet is D, etc; not very clever, and easily cracked, but adequate for a brief message.

All cryptography at the time used these same simple principles.

Although the British had a more than adequate knowledge of German ciphers in 1914, the problem was speed of decryption without mechanical or electronic aid.

Room 40 staffers had to work at their utmost speediness to decipher on a daily basis just a very few of the many hundreds of intercepted messages, using the *Handelsschiffsverkehrsbuch*, the Imperial German Naval Code book.

On 3rd August 1914, the cableship *Alert* cut Germany's five trans-Atlantic telegraph cables running through the English Channel, followed by the six cables connecting Britain and Germany.

The Royal Navy had one 'wireless station', in Stockton-on-

Sir James Alfred Ewing of Room 40.

Tees, which was capable of intercepting German radio messages. The Post Office and the Marconi Company were quick to add their manpower and professional skills – along with amateur radio hams and the staff and students of the Naval Colleges of Osborne and Dartmouth.

The random hotchpotch of the extravagant German Naval radio traffic gave vital information: a significant increase in the volume of certain signals, along with tell-tale clues within laboriously deciphered messages, could trigger Room 40 to advise the Admiralty to authorise a 'sweep'.

5

Ye Mariners of England
That guard our native seas,
Whose flag has braved, a thousand years,
The battle and the breeze –
Your glorious standard launch again
To match another foe!
And sweep through the deep,
While the stormy winds do blow, –
While the battle rages loud and long,
And the stormy winds do blow.
                    – Thomas Campbell c.1800

Should the intelligence gleaned by Room 40 have carried suffi-cient weight with the Admiralty, the Grand Fleet, already fully armed and fuelled with steam up, would be 'radioed', and would immediately set to sea at full ahead.

Hundreds of ships, from flocks of diminutive and lethally dainty destroyers to processions of giant steel castles of grey battleships, converged from Scapa Flow and the Firth of Forth at an agreed rendezvous – some hundred miles from the east coast of Scotland.

Through masterly seamanship, all ships settled into a prede-termined order of battle, and commenced a 'sweep' – a lethal net cast wide to ambush any elements of the German High

Seas Fleet which might have had the temerity to venture out of their heavily defended harbours of Kiel and Wilhelmshaven.

*   *   *

The Bolognese Guglielmo Giovanni Maria Marconi was born of an indigenous landowner and his Gaelic wife, Annie, daughter of Andrew Jameson of Daphne Castle, Wexford and granddaughter of John Jameson, the Scot who established the Irish whiskey industry in Dublin – in 1780.

Using the building block breakthroughs of Bell, Tainter, Hughes, Hertz, Edison, Maxwell, Faraday, Bose, Braun and the Serbian-American 'mad scientist' Tesla, the 20-year-old Marconi and his butler Mignani developed the principles of long distance 'wireless telegraphy' using 'morse code'.

By 1909 he was a Nobel Prize winner in physics.

In 1897 he had established 'The Wireless Telegraph and Signal Company in Britain', with offices on the Strand – now occupied by *Möet et Chandon*.

In 1902 the Marconi station in County Wexford, via a booster transmitter at Poldhu in Cornwall, had sent a radio message in morse to Signal Hill in St John's, Newfoundland – 2,200 miles away.

In 1903 the first Marconi radio message from the USA was sent as a greeting from President Theodore Roosevelt to King Edward VII.

On 15th April 1912, Marconi radio operators on RMS *Titanic* eventually communicated their distress to colleagues on RMS *Carpathia*, 58 miles away.

By 1914, Marconi's invention was in common usage: therefore *en clair* transmission was not an option for the military. Furthermore, decipherment was too long-winded for a fast

Guglielmo Marconi with some of his first telegraphs.

manoeuvring fleet at sea, especially in battle.

Sea conditions are notoriously unpredictable – totally fickle. The North Sea is particularly prone to storm tides and super-steep waves: shipping has always been endangered by its vast areas of shallows and shifting sand banks, and the dreaded *haar* – the sudden blinding sea fog.

Meteorology was in its infancy in the 1900s. The stimulus of *Titanic*'s disastrous collision with an aberrant iceberg, and the weather's seemingly unpredictable influence on gas warfare, artillery fire and the performance of the Zeppelin and aeroplane was not enough to overcome profound scientific ignorance
  – 'WYSIWYG'.

6

Offshore where the sea and skyline blend
In rain, the daylight dies;
The sullen, shouldering swells attend
Night and our sacrifice.
Adown the stricken capes no flare --
No mark on spit or bar, --
Girdled and desperate we dare
The blindfold game of war.

            – Rudyard Kipling, 1898

Encrypted radio messages through wireless telegraphy, 'W/T', alerted the Grand Fleet to assemble for battle with unprecedented speed. Once at sea, however, signalling was Nelsonian.

Captain Blackwood of HMS *Euryalis*, a frigate standing off Cadiz two days before Trafalgar, wrote: "Though our fleet was at sixteen leagues off, I have let Lord N. know of their coming out... at this moment we are within four miles of the Enemy, and talking to Lord Nelson by means of Sir H. Popham's signals, though so distant, but repeated along by the rest of the frigates of this Squadron."

Home Riggs Popham, fifteenth child of the British Consul at Tétouan in Morocco, Westminster and Trinity, Cambridge – early naval scientist and enthusiastic entrepreneur – half-inched the French Naval numerical flag code.

By 1800, he had developed the world's first alphabetic signalling system: thus, "England expects…"; and, by 1813, the Popham Code contained 6000 phrases and 60,000 words. The 'International Code of Signals', as Popham's invention was renamed in 1870, is still in effective use today.

In 1914, the practice of flag signalling from mast to mast, from ship to shore, had remained unchanged since Trafalgar.

At sea, the Admiral's hoist of flags was repeated from ship to ship within the Grand Fleet. Many hundreds of shivering junior officers, peering through fogged binoculars from wildly swaying foretops, would anxiously watch, and shout frantically translated orders through their voice pipes to the bridges, the command centres of their respective captains.

All ships of the Fleet would have been required to repeat immediately the flag messages in confirmation of their receipt, and to act in common accord within the prescribed ten minutes.

In order to achieve speedy conformity in fleet manoeuvres involving hundreds of ships of all sizes and purposes, the visibility of flags was of paramount importance. Big ships had big flags; little ships, smaller flags.

Capital ships sailed in three parallel rows to enhance diagonal sight lines.

But, if visibility was impaired by the prevailing fogs and foul weather of the North Sea, there were serious problems.

As encrypted W/T was impracticable at sea in battle conditions, the only other available signalling methods were semaphore and lamp.

Semaphore, using hand-held flags, was only useful at very short range, but the new and powerful Aldis lamp – the original 'searchlight' – using a shutter system and the carbon arc to

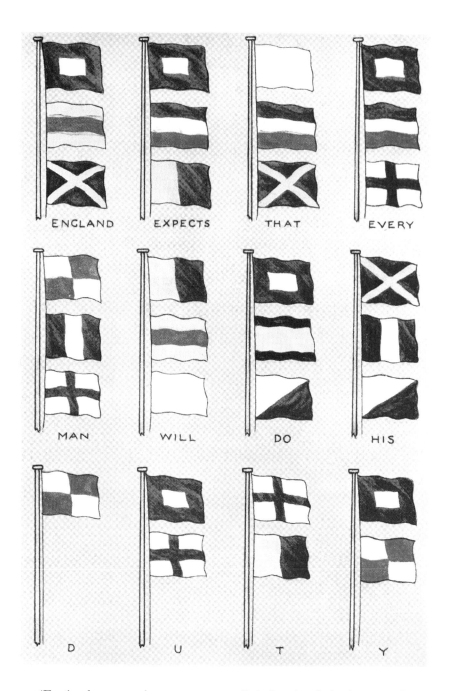

'England expects that every man will do his duty', the last signal from Admiral Nelson at the Battle of Trafalgar, 1805.

Training Ship *Mercury* at flag semaphore instruction.

transmit morse code messages, was as effective in daylight as in night time fleet communication.

Nevertheless, even the most massive capital ship could become invisible within fret, foam, fog and monstrous swell – and, indeed, in the smoke of battle.

7

There's something in a flying horse,
There's something in a huge balloon;
But through the clouds I'll never float
Until I have a little Boat,
Shaped like the crescent-moon,
And now I 'have' a little Boat,
In shape a very crescent-moon
Fast through the clouds my boat can sail;
But if perchance your faith should fail,
Look up -- and you shall see me soon!
The woods, my Friends, are round you roaring,
Rocking and roaring like a sea;
The noise of danger's in your ears
And ye have all a thousand fears
Both for my little Boat and me!
                    – William Wordsworth, 1798

The Montgolfier brothers launched the first human flight in their hot air balloon, suspending a 'gondola', a 'little Boat', in 1783: it was made of taffeta, sackcloth and paper, all bright paint and gilt, lifted by a fire producing a gas that they called 'levity'.

It was an utter sensation.

Ten days later, the Robert brothers flew the first hydrogen balloon. The following year they launched an elongated elliptical

Vue d'optique shows the balloon launched by the Montgolfier brothers ascending from the Palace of Versailles, France, before the royal family, 19th September, 1783.

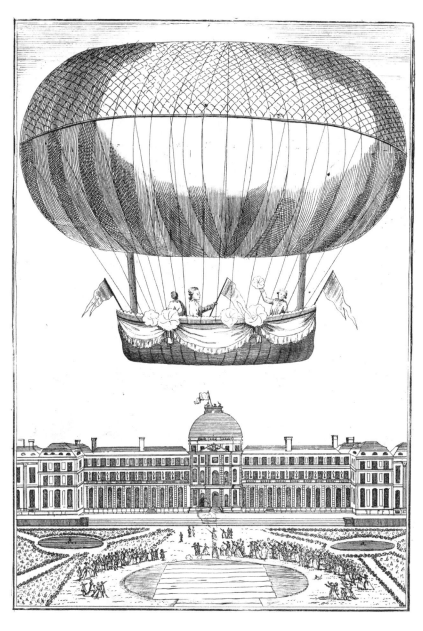

Anne-Jean and Marie-Noël Robert riding in the gondola of a
balloon ascending from the Tuileries Garden, Paris, France,
19th September, 1784.

version, a skyship, powered and steered by oars and umbrellas: it was called 'a dirigible' – *un directible.*

Its launch in Paris was watched by 400,000 people, including Benjamin Franklin. Landing 21 kilometres away, it was destroyed by 'terrified peasants' with pitchforks.

The dirigible carried the first scientific instruments to rise above the earth's surface.

Today we fly the tiny celebratory kongming lanterns – invented for military signalling in the Shu Han Kingdom of China, in the third century AD.

*   *   *

The practicality of 'lighter than air' craft was enabled by the German invention of 'duralumin', an alloy of aluminium with copper, manganese and magnesium, which gave rigid strength to the levity of the parent element.

Count Ferdinand von Zeppelin had knowledge of this ultra-secret process, and designed around it a giant airship powered by the new internal combustion engine.

After exorbitant personal and public investment and a number of dramatic failures, the *Luftschiffbau Zeppelin GmbH* and the Zeppelin Foundation were established – the 'zeppelin' had become a German national enthusiasm.

By 1914, DELAG, *Deutsche Luftschiffahrts - Aktiengesellschaft*, the world's first commercial airline, had carried 34,000 passengers in seven zeppelins flying over 1,500 flights.

In this form, the zeppelin was 160 metres long with a volume of $25,000m^3$. It could carry 9000kg, and was powered by three Maybach engines enabling a maximum speed of 80 kph (50 mph).

The buoyant 'flammable air' which gave lift to the zeppelin

Zeppelin airship ZRIII at hanger in Friedrichshaven in preparation
for its first test flight.

had been identified by Henry Cavendish in 1766. Lavoisier gave it the name of 'hydrogen' in 1783.

Hydrogen was created in the 18th century by a process that involved pouring 'a quarter of a tonne of sulphuric acid onto half a tonne of white hot scrap iron' to produce 35 m³ of gas capable of lifting 9kg.

During the American Civil War of the 1860s, portable compact hydrogen gas generators were developed to fly the observation balloons of the Union Army.

Storage of the gas was an entirely different problem.

No material known to man was impermeable to hydrogenous gas other than the mammalian intestine – for obvious reasons: it was also well-known that the fart is highly flammable.

Today, BMW, *Bayerische Motoren Werke AG*, is working on a practicable liquid hydrogen tank for its cars: in 1914, it was imperative to von Zeppelin that there were 'gasbags' for his airships.

In 1862 chloroform was stored for inhalable anaesthesia in goldbeater's skin bags. The astonishingly thin goldbeater's skin is made from the elastic and durable cured guts of cattle, with the original purpose of producing micro-thin gold leaf – it withstood much heavy thrashing, interleaved with fine sheets of the pure metal.

"A pack of 1000 pieces of goldbeater's skin requires the gut of about 400 oxen and is only one inch thick".

Within the bowels of the outer structure of the rigid duralumin skeleton of the gigantic zeppelin were multiples of independent gas bags – 'cells'. To make these cells, 200,000 sheets of skin were required for each zeppelin, representing the intestines of 80,000 oxen.

In the 1880s, the Alsatian Weinling family had been employed by the Royal Engineers at Chatham to make the unique gut gas bags for their observation balloons. By 1912 the German government had expropriated the secret process.

An entirely successful British rigid dirigible airship – a zeppelin – has yet to be launched.

By 1915 German zeppelins were bombing London.

The night raids were aimed at military sites around the Thames Estuary, but after the introduction of the 'blackout', they were random, and more irritating than harmful.

The Kaiser had forbidden attacks west of the Tower of London, "for fear of harming his dear cousins".

British weather thwarted most raids, but panicky civilian concerns generated new and energetic defences – anti-aircraft guns, search lights and night fighters – all of which were relatively ineffective, but made a 'priceless show'.

However, on 3rd September 1916 *Schütte-Lanz* SL.II, having bombed South Mimms and Ponders End, was attacked at 2.15 am by Lt. William Leefe Robinson Royal Flying Corps at 12,000 feet. Thousands of Londoners cheered as the gigantic silver cigar, triangulated by many bright beams, burst into a spectacular fireball, and crashed in a field behind the Plough Inn at Cuffley.

Lt. Robinson was awarded the VC.

After maltreatment as a prisoner of war, he died of Spanish 'flu in 1918, aged 23.

*   *   *

Dropping light showers of little bombs on the suburbs of London was not about to change the course of the Great War. But the 16 zeppelins of the German Navy were a truly formidable threat: two or more patrolled the North Sea at any one time,

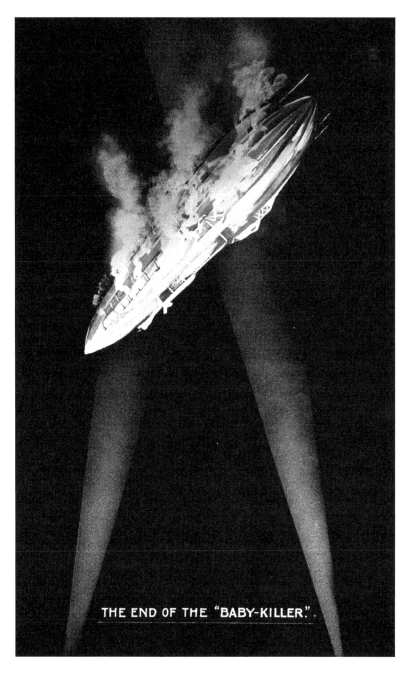

Schütte-Lanz SL.II.

RAF Flying-Boat F2a Type.

keenly watching for any approach of the British Grand Fleet and its disposition, or any mine-laying activity, using W/T to report to *der Deutschen Hochseeflotte*.

The Royal Navy had no countermeasure.

The zeppelin flew high, and ships' infant anti-aircraft gunnery did not have the accuracy or reach to cause it serious harm.

The new British 'sea planes' were hurried into service, carried aboard converted merchant ships, but they were excessively difficult to launch and retrieve, and were, being underpowered, too slow to ascend to an attacking height.

And, contrary to any preconceptions, it proved exceptionally difficult to ignite the zeppelins' supposedly highly flammable hydrogen cells. Bullets and shrapnel fragments might puncture a few individual gas bags, but the small wounds would only cause a fractional loss of lift, and would not generate sufficient heat to ignite the hydrogen within.

8

Hush, hush! Tread softly! Hush, hush my dear!
Tho' your feet are more light than a fairy's feet,
Who dances on bubbles where brooklets meet...
— John Keats, 1818

Born of desperation and urgent necessity, 'hush hush stunts' were conceived.

Incendiary ammunition was secretly perfected. The bullets contained phosphorus, and they burnt furiously and briefly, leaving a blue smoke 'trace': at short range they were lethally effective – now hydrogen in gas bags exploded into near-invisible blue flames with satisfactory alacrity.

So hideous were the human wounds caused by phosphorus that the use of 'tracer bullets' was strictly limited to attacks on the 'gas chambers' of observation balloons and zeppelins. Pilots were required to carry written orders to this effect.

As zeppelin design became more sophisticated – achieving speeds of 80 mph, payloads of 3 to 4 tons at heights of up to 25,000 feet and a range of 4,000 miles – the British were increasingly unable to meet the threat.

Patently, the zeppelin's bombing capability was inconsequential, but the all-seeing 'eye in the sky' was intolerable; no Allied aeroplane could reach its operating altitude, and, over the North Sea, it had a panoramic view of any noteworthy activity.

Handley-Page 0/400 – the 'bloody paralyser'.

Commander Charles Samson, Royal Naval Air Service,
with beard, 1914.

Several bombing attempts were made by the Royal Naval Air Service, the RNAS, on the zeppelin sheds at Cuxhaven and Wilhelmshaven with limited success. The tiny seaplane 'bombers' flying with minute bomblets at extreme range had impossible missions.

Powerful twin-engine bombers were not available until late 1916. The RNAS flew the Handley-Page 0/100 on its first raid on 16th March 1917.

The RNAS had commissioned Sir Frederick Handley Page to design this heavy bomber to be a 'Bloody Paralyser of an aeroplane', to attack the zeppelin yards, and ultimately to make revenge attacks on Berlin.

Between times the British Grand Fleet had no 'far-reaching eyes': first contact with Hun ships was made by the fast moving screen of light cruisers and destroyers; nor did it have a means of deterring the lurking dirigible.

*   *   *

The first man to take off from a ship under way was Commander Charles Samson – in 1912. His feat was achieved by fitting the gun turret of a large ship with a removable wooden 'flying-off platform' extending over the long barrels.

The ship steamed into the wind: the speed of the ship, and maximum power from the aircraft's engine, hopefully generated sufficient lift for take off.

Of course, having successfully become airborne, and having completed a mission, the problem remained of how to 'land'.

In the midst of the North Sea, land was remote – Scotland to the west, Denmark to the east: the only alternative was to 'ditch in the drink'.

These seaborne 'kites', soon to be permanent assets attached

Aeroplanes on forward deck of HMS *Furious*.

to every capital ship, constituted the sole British opposition to the zeppelin threat.

Aircraft were becoming more reliable and their weaponry more effective. But the means of launching and landing them at sea was unacceptably wasteful of men and *matériel*.

Covertly, HMS *Furious*, one of Fisher's most secret battle cruisers, already in the course of construction, was tentatively modified – the first ship to be capable of launching *and* landing aeroplanes with wheels.

Air power had begun its ascendancy.

9

O Fortune, who dost bestow the throne's high boon with mocking hand, in dangerous and doubtful state thou settest the too exalted. Never have sceptres obtained calm peace or certain tenure; care on care wears them down, and ever do fresh storms vex their souls.

– Seneca, 55 BC

During the inconclusive but bruising Battle of Jutland, fought on 31st May and 1st June 1916 – the one and only major clash of arms between the two fleets – the tender HMS *Engadine* was ordered to launch one of its four Short 184 'floatplanes' to confirm the sighting of German ships.

This was the first time that a heavier-than-air aircraft had been flown in a sea battle.

Sadly, the Aldis lamp signal reporting the successful reconnaissance failed to be picked up due to poor visibility.

This was just one example of the critical lack of communication between British ships that had allowed the Imperial High Seas Fleet to escape during the night.

*   *   *

As the German surface fleet had proved to be impotent, the Kaiser authorised unrestricted submarine warfare – in overt contravention of the Hague Conventions.

In January 1917 Germany declared the seas around Britain

HMS *Queen Mary* sinking at Jutland, 1916.

British seaplane carrier HMS *Engadine*.

and its allies a war zone: all ships of any nationality, neutral or not, became targets for the proliferating fleet of U-boats – *die Unterseeboote* – commonly called 'baby killers'.

The sinking of the luxury passenger liner RMS *Lusitania* by U-20 in 1915, a much adulated military feat in Germany, had already irritated America – of the 1,198 civilians who drowned, 128 had been US citizens.

*   *   *

The devastating loss of life on the Western Front during the protracted Battle of the Somme and von Falkenhayn's meat grinding Siege of Verdun was fast exhausting German and Allied military energies.

The British naval blockade of German ports was leading to significant civilian food shortages, severe rationing and riots. The Hun generals and politicians convinced themselves that the risk of drawing America into the war was worth taking – that, within five months, an all-out U-boat offensive could sink sufficient tonnage, much of it inevitably American, to starve Britain in its turn into surrender.

The 'Zimmermann telegram' from the German Foreign Secretary inviting Mexico to conspire against the United States was deciphered by Room 40.

On 6th April 1917, America entered the war.

*   *   *

Initially, as predicted by von Tirpitz, German submarines caused serious havoc, sinking a quarter of incoming merchant shipping. Following a vicious bout of internecine conflict within the Admiralty and an anxious government, the Royal Navy was persuaded to re-introduce the 18th-century notion

Sinking of SS *Lusitania*, illustration from *La Domenica del Corriere*,
7th June, 1915.

British troops of the Border Regiment resting in 'funk' holes during
the Battle of the Somme, August 1916.

A British convoy steering a zig-zag course in the danger zone.

of the convoy system – a flock of lumbering laden freighters shepherded by a defensive screen of fighting ships.

This tactic was again exceptionally effective: thereafter, only 154 of the 16,539 ships convoyed across the Atlantic were sunk.

The Hun's last throw, the gamble of an overwhelming submarine assault, had spectacularly failed.

*   *   *

British 'blimps' – small non-rigid rotund balloon airships – had been developed to patrol coastal waters. The RNAS used them for spotting mines and submarines with a cold crew of ten in an open cockpit, five machine guns, six 230lb bombs, and an endurance of at least 24 hours.

By 2013 marine archaeologists had identified 41 WWI U-boat wrecks along the eastern English coast. In all, 187 of the 380 strong German submarine fleet had been sunk.

Obviously this British 'blimp' was more effective than the archetypal fat, florid and fatuous colonel of the Second World War.

*   *   *

American supplies and, above all, troops and munitions, flooded into Europe.

But the Russians had capitulated, and Germany could now concentrate all its remaining strength on the Western Front.

The Hun needed to act with alacrity and full and mighty force if it was to break through Allied defences before American military and logistical strength could be widely deployed.

The Spring Offensive of 1918, the Kaiser's Battle, *der Kaiserschlacht*, was ill-planned. The main thrust was intended to outflank the British holding the ground between the River

British Airship No. 37, a 'blimp', escorting a convoy.

Arrival of the first American contingents in France,
Saint-Nazaire, late June, 1917.

The Menin Road, 1919, Paul Nash.

Somme and the English Channel.

The British army withdrew into pre-planned defensive positions around Amiens, and the German élite storm troopers charged into a vacuum – a derelict, war-wasted, valueless land – a tactic borrowed from Wellington.

A sufficiency of horse-drawn supplies, food and ammunition, could not reach the depleting German army through the roadless, shell-churned earth.

After a few days the offensive was brought to a halt by the German High Command. But not before the opponents had lost a further half million men.

The Allies, bolstered now by fresh Yankee divisions, launched their counter attack: the 'Hundred Days Offensive' started on 8th August 1918.

The German army made a bravura fighting retreat, but its position was hopeless.

The Central Powers requested an armistice.

The humiliating conditions put forward by US President Woodrow Wilson, the 'Fourteen Points', were reluctantly accepted, but not before socialist rebellion and the abdication of Kaiser Wilhelm II, German Emperor, King of Prussia.

The Armistice came into effect at 11am on 11th November 1918.

The Central Powers – the German Empire, the Austro-Hungarian Empire, the Ottoman Empire, the Kingdom of Bulgaria – had ceased to exist

– 'like a dream was obliterated'.

IO

It might have appeared to all involved that this was to be the inexorable dénouement, the fatal final act – but not to Admiral Franz Ritter von Hipper, the son of a Bavarian Catholic shop-keeper, now Commander of *der Kaiserliche Marine*, the German Imperial Navy.

Without any authorisation from a superior, Hipper, whose motive was said to have been to improve somehow the German hand in the Armistice negotiations, planned a suicidal attack on the British Grand Fleet.

All available ships from Kiel and Wilhelmshaven, on his orders, were to break out and confront *der Engländer – der Inselaffe*, 'the island ape' – and, through elaborate deceptions, destroy it in its English Channel.

*   *   *

Admiral Franz Ritter von Hipper.

Mutiny of the High Seas Fleet. Gustav Noske, appointed as
Military Governor by the Workers and Soldiers Council of Kiel,
addresses submarine crews.

Since the Battle of Jutland, the great capital ships of the Imperial High Seas Fleet had been demeaningly confined to their harbours, festering in their berths, gathering weed and barnacle, whilst the best of their seamen leeched away into the more prestigious submarine service. With the declining fortunes of Germany, those crews that remained became increasingly ill-fed, disillusioned and disaffected.

On the receipt of the order of 24th October 1918 to prepare for this futile mission, the sailors of the Imperial Fleet mutinied. Some were shot by firing squad, others were imprisoned.

Mutinies and mass protests for *Frieden und Brot*, 'freedom and bread', rapidly conflated into overt countrywide rebellion.

The harbours of Kiel and Wilhelmshaven were in the control of tens of thousands of revolutionaries. Socialist activists, mimicking their Russian Bolshevist counterparts, formed Workers' and Soldiers' Councils: military discipline was defunct.

The Red flag was flown and anarchy prevailed.

By 11th November 1918, no German ship was fit to fight – nor indeed, perhaps to sail.

*   *   *

On the spanking smart tender to the flagship of the Grand Fleet, the petite and elegant destroyer HMS *Oak*, its hull glistening in bright enamel, flying the royal standard, King George V sailed to review the greatest concentration of capital ships ever assembled.

Admiral Sir David Beatty, Commander-in-Chief of the Grand Fleet, the youngest Admiral since Nelson, the dashing "new Nelson", saluted from the Atlantic grey leviathan, HMS *Queen Elizabeth*.

Tiered ranks of many hundreds of ships of the Allied Grand

HM King George V with the Commander of the Grand Fleet,
Admiral Sir David Beatty.

HMS *Queen Elizabeth*.

The Grand Fleet in the Firth Of Forth.

Fleet lined the Firth of Forth on 20th November 1918.

Included was Battleship Division Nine: the coal-burning US ships *New York*, *Wyoming*, *Florida* and *Delaware* had struggled across the Atlantic through ferocious storms to become the Sixth Battle Squadron.

The following day the assembled Grand Fleet was due to receive into captivity the Imperial High Seas Fleet – its elusive foe.

*   *   *

An intransigent Admiral Beatty had delivered the Allied ultimatum that, should the German High Seas Fleet not surrender itself by 21st November, Heligoland would be re-occupied.[2]

Britain had ceded these islands to Germany in 1890: they commanded access to the North Sea and the vital Baltic Sea link of the Kiel Canal.

If non-compliant, Germany would be subject to an ever more stringent blockade.

The 'Republic of Germany' was declared on 9th November 1918, but it was Leading Stoker Bernhard Kuhnt who was the illiterate President of the 'Republic of Oldenburg-East Frisia' – elected by the sailors and marines of the vestigial crews of the Imperial High Seas Fleet.

Commissioned officers were stripped of their badges of rank and deprived of any executive power. Ward rooms were abandoned to brothels and bars.

Despite the absence of any form of discipline, through some innate social conscience, a sufficient number of sober and sane

---

2. Twenty-two years later, a Nazi labour camp on the island of Alderney, the Channel Island which commands the French coast, was to be named, with pointed irony, 'Heligoland'.

Admiral of the Fleet John Rushworth Jellicoe, First Earl Jellicoe.

sailors remained to prepare the High Seas Fleet for its final voyage to the humiliation of surrender and incarceration.

The alternative, the oblivion of their new German State, *der Vaterland,* was too dreadful for them to contemplate.

The young turk Beatty and his predecessor, the old-school Admiral of the Fleet John Rushworth Jellicoe, First Earl Jellicoe, had succeeded in emasculating an adolescent but truly formidable German sea power, but the struggle had ended before submarine warfare had been fully examined.

The question was to be revisited shortly.

II

But whether in calm or wrack-wreath, whether by dark or day,
I heave them whole to the conger or rip their plates away,
First of the scattered legions, under a shrieking sky,
Dipping between the rollers, the English Flag goes by.
            – Rudyard Kipling, 1891

The German flag will be hauled down at sunset today, Thursday,
and will not be hoisted again without permission.
            – Admiral Sir David Beatty, 21st November 1918

The superior ammunition and the secret gunnery instrumentation which had seriously embarrassed the British ships at the Battle of Jutland, were dumped unceremoniously on the quaysides of Kiel and Wilhelmshaven.

Food filled the ammunition lockers, and all guns were rendered inoperable.

This very public shaming of the new-born German nation and its *Kultur* cut deep.

The splendid German Army was, by way of Article 61 of the Imperial Constitution, subject to the Prussian military code. Accordingly, in the officers' manual of 1902, "the laws of war on land" stipulated that "an energetically conducted war cannot be carried on solely against the combatant enemy and his defences, but extends and should extend to the destruction of his material and moral resources. Humanitarian considerations, such as respect for persons and property, can be taken into consideration only provided that the nature and object of the war adopt themselves to that course".

The militaristic Prussian land-owning *noblesse*, the all-powerful *Junkers*, underpinned every subsequent régime until decimated by Hitler following the failed assassination attempt of 1944.

Communist ideology was perceived to have been the brainchild of the Jewish intelligentsia, embodied in the persona of the Bolshevist-Marxist Leon Trotsky, born Lev Davidovich Bronshtein in 1879, the founder and first leader of the Red Army.

The Prussian *Junkers*, and subsequently Adolf Hitler and his Nazi Party, continued to regard the Jews as their natural enemies.

*   *   *

Hipper had no wish to lead the surrender of his depleted and decrepit fleet of 70 serviceable ships. He delegated the humiliation to his junior colleague Rear-Admiral Ludwig von Reuter.

On 21st November, as agreed, and greatly to the relief of the Grand Fleet who had anticipated a last ditch fight, the still lethal remnants of the Imperial High Seas Fleet loomed at half ahead through the eerie silence of a morning mist and a glassy sea.

The decks of the rusting hulks were strewn with soiled and sullen sailors bearing their signature red armbands. They were greeted by 370 Allied ships with every gun loaded, and every crew tense at their battle stations.

The Hun ships were escorted to the Firth of Forth, and corralled – boxed in on four sides by overwhelming fire power.

Between 25th and 27th November they were moved to Scapa Flow for internment.

Rear-Admiral Ludwig von Reuter.

German battleships at Scapa Flow.

SMS *Bremse* at Scapa Flow.

German destroyers at Scapa Flow.

HMS *Tiger* at Scapa Flow.

The incarcerated skeleton crews included *ci-devant* officers, "dumb with shame", whilst their wonderfully conceived war-machines descended into "indescribable filth".

The Scottish conditions in the ensuing months were cold, cruel and intolerable – inadequate and tedious food and total lack of discipline and recreation – a misery marginally alleviated by liberal quantities of cheap Admiralty brandy.

Despite close supervision, von Reuter and his crews had devised an intrigue to defeat the Allies' intention of profiting from their valuable spoils of war.

At a predetermined flag signal, the German crews of the High Seas Fleet opened their seacocks and scuttled their ships.

Within five hours on 21st June, 1919 most of the Fleet were irretrievably immersed in the deep waters of Scapa Flow.

1,774 German sailors were picked up and made prisoners-of-war: nine had died.

Their turnkey, Vice-Admiral Sir Sydney Fremantle, was professionally piqued, but admitted to his colleagues, "I could not resist feeling some sympathy for von Reuter, who had preserved his dignity when placed against his will in a highly unpleasant and invidious position."

Rear-Admiral Ludwig von Reuter was repatriated in January 1920 – welcomed home as the hero who had saved the honour of the Imperial High Seas Fleet.

The archetypal Prussian *Junker*, von Reuter was resurrected from obscurity and promoted to full Admiral by Adolf Hitler in 1939.

But, unlike Hipper, Scheer, Tirpitz, Graf Spee and Bismarck, Reuter's name was not to be commemorated in the new capital ships of the Nazi *Kriegsmarine*.

Scuttling of German battleship SMS *Bayern* at
Scapa Flow, 21st June, 1919.

12

The nation must be taught to bear losses. No amount of skill on the part of the higher commanders, no training, however good, on the part of the officers and men, no superiority of arms and ammunition, however great, will enable victories to be won without the sacrifice of men's lives. The nation must be prepared to see heavy casualty lists.

– Field Marshal Douglas Haig, July 1916

Figures are difficult to come by, but it is estimated that Britain lost 35,970 aircraft in the Great War – only around 4,000 in combat. 16,620 aircrew were killed, wounded or missing.

Evidently accidents were commonplace, killing many more pilots than bullets.

The French invention of the seaplane in 1910 had generated an investigatory 'Air Department' in the Admiralty.

The Royal Naval Air Service became independent of the Royal Flying Corps on 1st August, 1915: it had a staff of 720, flying 93 assorted aeroplanes and six airships.

In 1910 the exclusive and wealthy Royal Aero Club had donated two aeroplanes to the Royal Navy, along with the services of its members as instructors and the use of its aerodrome at Eastchurch on the Isle of Sheppey in Kent. It was stipulated that the trainee pilots were to be unmarried, and were able to pay the membership fees of the Club.

Field Marshal Sir Douglas Haig.

Remind yourself that Louis Blériot had, to much astonishment, flown the English Channel on 25th July, 1909, in an aeroplane of his own design.

When the RNAS merged with the Royal Flying Corps to form the Royal Air Force in April 1918, it sported 55,066 officers and men, 2,949 aeroplanes, 103 airships and 126 airstations.

*   *   *

The Royal Navy is the Senior Service, established long before any concept of a standing army. Its officers were promoted through personal recommendation, inherent aptitude and strict examination – not by purchase or privilege.

Its ranks were filled with skilled and disciplined seamen, melded into self-dependent teams – 'crews'. For more than three centuries, these fiercely proud and competitive units had co-operated to form, when necessary, 'fleets'

Forceful, perceptive and charismatic personalities with quick intelligence were required to forge these highly individualistic and eccentric elements into effective weapons of war.

Nelson had been the epitome of an admiral – dashing, daring and adequately wounded in his juniority – later a caring, insightful and highly competent commander. He was the sixth child of eleven born to a Norfolk parson.

His sailors wept at his death.

A hundred years on, his lustre lingered. Less gifted successors lazed in his wake, many languishing in the lush outposts of Empire, enjoying the easements of unchallenged supremacy.

Happily somebody had remained alert at home – the duo of the youthful political First Lord of the Admiralty, Winston Churchill, and the septuagenarian First Sea Lord, 'Jacky' Fisher – who had replaced flotillas of ancient rust buckets with Fisher's

Churchill as First Lord of the Admiralty.

Soldiers in the grounds of the 4th London General Hospital.

ferociously powerful dreadnought battleships and his hard-hitting 'greyhounds', the battlecruisers. – 'the Splendid Cats'.

*   *   *

By 1915 the brutal human wastage of trench warfare had started to seep into the public consciousness. The limbless, mutilated youths in blue 'hospital suits' were increasingly evident, hobbling on every high street.

Women's use of the 'white feather' – for cowardice – ceased.

The strident belligerency of the early months moderated as the mortality rate rose alarmingly, and conscription, having been introduced in 1916, became inclusive of married men and of men up to the age of 51.

There had been no hero of the hour – no Wellington, no Nelson – no sweeping victories for Britain – no apparent saviour in this endless drudge of horror.

France was fast descending into chaos and rebellion.

Tottering Germany had simply been the first to blink – unable and unwilling to face up to the industrial might and the new world vigour of America.

Field Marshal Douglas Haig had regarded himself as God's servant, but became vilified as 'Butcher Haig'.

More than two million British servicemen became casualties under his command.

Forward Joe Soap's army, marching without fear,
With our old commander, safely in the rear.
He boasts and skites from morn till night,
And thinks he's very brave,
But the men who really did the job are dead and in their grave.
Forward Joe Soap's army, marching without fear,
With our old commander, safely in the rear.[3]
       – Anon, to the theme of *Onward Christian Soldiers*

*   *   *   *

The Commander-in-Chief of the Grand Fleet at the Battle of Jutland had been Admiral of the Fleet John Rushworth Jellicoe, First Earl Jellicoe, son of a captain in the Royal Mail Steam Packet Company.

He had made no serious mistakes, but the German High Seas Fleet had escaped, having done some serious damage between times, and there was a countrywide sense of disappointment: the defeat of the Hun navy could have ended the war.

Jellicoe was promoted to First Sea Lord, the most senior sailor, where he came to be seen as the eternal pessimist, and was removed.

His place as Commander-in-Chief of the Grand Fleet was taken by David Richard Beatty, First Earl Beatty – a battle cruiser captain, a cat captain through and through – handsome, smart, aggressive, predatory, the illegitimate child of an Irish cavalry officer: he had had little in the way of a formal education.

3. 'Joe' = an ordinary person – 'soap' = rhyming slang for dope, a dumb person – 'skite' = to drink heavily – 'Our old commander' = Field Marshal Douglas Haig, First Earl Haig of Bemersyde.

Beatty on the bridge of HMS *Queen Elizabeth.*

Early well-publicised successes in China and the Sudan and inherent charm propelled him into English society. He met an American billionairess whilst hunting, married her and became impermeably independent.

From his flagship HMS *Queen Elizabeth*, Beatty, having presided over the surrender of the German High Seas Fleet, was soon to be promoted, in his turn, to First Sea Lord.

Further advancement was blocked: Leo Amery, the Colonial Secretary, an indecently bright contemporary of Winston Churchill at Harrow, refused to approve his appointment as Governor General of Canada as "he had no manners and an impossible American wife".

Amery had been born in Gorakhpur, the son of an officer in the Indian Forestry Commission and a Hungarian Jewish mother of considerable intellect.

Of course, the young officers of the Grand Fleet thought hugely well of Beatty – his charisma arose from undeniable derring-do, Gaelic arrogance, newly acquired wealth, dashing good looks and a creative tailor.

He was intensely disappointed not to have had his own Trafalgar.

The Grand Fleet were pleased to see him on his bridge on 21st November 1918.

13

If I should come out of this war alive, I will have more luck than brains.

– Manfred Albrecht Freiherr von Richthofen,
'the Red Baron', *Kaput* 21st April 1918

The yo-yo is very difficult to explain. It was first perfected by the well-known Chinese fighter pilot Yo-Yo Noritake. He also found it difficult to explain, being quite devoid of English.

– Squadron Leader KG Holland, RAF, 1940

I will leave it to my father to describe his experiences.

But, of the 23 teenagers who entered 'RNAS Training Establishment Cranwell', only three survived the ensuing nine months: this he doesn't mention. The trio wrote letters to each other every Christmas thereafter.

It is interesting to note that they flew 'BE2C's' and 'BE2E's' at Cranwell: the prefix 'BE' stands for *Blériot Experimental*.

Of course, the aeroplanes that they flew were prototypes – the Sopwith Pup and Camel, the Bristol Bullet, the Nieuports 10 and 12; all were being 'tried out' by the novice pilots.

Early aeroplanes were powered by 'pusher' engines behind the pilot. The later 'tractor' engine in front of the pilot, being 'rotary', exerted powerful 'torque' on the flimsy fuselage, the

The end of a spin.

Harry Hawker.

whole engine block turning with the propeller acting as a giant gyroscope.

The newbie pilot only had to apply a touch too much right rudder to send his 'kite' into an irreversible corkscrew 'spin', spiralling vertically into hard earth – or sea.

Annoyingly, too much left rudder tended to retard the fuel supply. Usually a quick dive could restart the engine, but not always.

Spins were usually fatal.

The emigrant Australian chauffeur Harry Hawker was employed by the aeroplane entrepreneur Tom Sopwith as a mechanic in 1912. A natural born aviator, he was soon promoted to chief test pilot.

One day in 1915, over Brooklands, the requisitioned car racing circuit, later the home of 'the Bentley Boys', Hawker intentionally put his Sopwith biplane into a spin. Using a technique suggested by a mathematical theory proposed by the German physicist Frederick Lindemann[4] of the Royal Aircraft Factory, he was able to recover.

His achievement was slow to filter through to the flying schools.

Hawker is better known today for his company's product, the Hawker 'Hurricane'.

*   *   *

The rotary engine was lubricated by adding castor oil to the fuel-air mixture. This was discharged in the exhaust fumes: when inhaled and ingested by the pilot it would cause chronic

---

4. Frederick Lindemann, First Viscount Cherwell (1886-1957), 'Baron Berlin', scientific advisor to Winston Churchill, advocate of 'area bombing' of German cities during World War II.

diarrhoea, and, despite protective cowling, the pilot was thoroughly drenched in flammable fluid.

The average life expectancy of a pilot on the Western Front was said to be 11 days.

They carried no parachutes.

What a way to die, to be sizzled alive or to jump and fall thousands of feet. I wonder if you are conscious all the way down? I'd much prefer a bullet through the head and have done with it.

– RFC Pilot Arthur Gould Lee

The fire phobic Irish 'Ace' Major 'Mick' Mannock VC DSO MC[5] always carried his service revolver. He died in a flaming aeroplane on 6th July 1918. It was thought he might have jumped – his revolver had not been fired, and he was found 250 yards from his wreck.

What the hell is wrong with those callous dolts at home that they won't give them to us?
– RFC Pilot Arthur Gould Lee, 3rd January 1918

Calthrop's 'Guardian Angel', a free fall parachute, was tested successfully in 1917.

No order for them was made until September 1918.

---

5. Edward Mannock (1887-1918), attributed with 58 victories, awarded the Victoria Cross posthumously. His medals were sold by his alcoholic father for £5.

Major 'Mick' Mannock VC DSO MC.

Calthrop's *Guardian Angel* patent.

14

Enjoy yourself, it's later than you think
Enjoy yourself, while you're still in the pink
The years go by, as quickly as you wink
Enjoy yourself, enjoy yourself
It's later than you think.
– Carl Sigman and Herb Magidson, 1949

On the land based air stations, RNAS pilots observed naval formalities: they saluted the quarter deck, attended divisions, slept in cabins and went ashore.

At sea, they were lucky to be on capital ships whose guns were long enough for them to 'take off'. These steel sea-monsters were better able to batter their way through the steep North Sea waves, but water inevitably found its way through innumerable vents, and swilled around decks at every level.

They might have been cold and wet and often frightened, but the teenage pilots were not necessarily always that miserable: 'Navy strength' Plymouth Gin is 57% alcohol by volume (today lager is around 5% abv, vodka 40%).

All wars have been fought on copious amounts of alcohol: life becomes more acceptable, senses somewhat benumbed, and the many extra hundreds of concentrated calories support gen-

Pink gins in the wardroom.

THE

WAR PLEDGE

I *promise, to abstain from the use of all Intoxicating Liquors while the War lasts.*

Name

Date

C.E T,S Depot, 89, Southampton Row, W.C.

'The King's Pledge' card.

eration of body heat in the cold, and maximal energy output under extreme physical duress.

Naval authorities encouraged "the moderate intake of a stimulant" – every pilot carried a 'hip flask'.

'Gin and tonic' was an Indian Army inspiration – a tastier and jollier way of taking a bitter daily dose of the anti-malarial quinine.

But carrying multiple small glass bottles of carbonated tonic water in storm tossed ships was not an option.

Venezuelan Angostura Bitters, a tincture of gentian, was a well-known sea sickness remedy, but was vile to swallow: a 'dash' or two in a tot or two of juniper based Plymouth Gin with a twist of lime or lemon was the ubiquitous Naval ward room panacea, 'Pink Gin'.

Drunkenness among the emancipated female war workers with new found wages to spend had become rife – the first ladettes had found their feet.

The government was profoundly worried. The Welsh Baptist Prime Minister Lloyd George opined that Britain was "fighting Germans, Austrians and Drink, and as far as I can see the greatest of these foes is Drink".

He promoted 'The King's Pledge' not to drink alcohol until the war was over. This conceit was not spectacularly successful, but the imposition of strict pub opening hours, punitive alcohol taxation and extortionate fines were more so.

Nevertheless, the free daily ration of alcohol continued to flow unabatedly to the military.

15

There were no restraints in France; these boys had money to spend and knew that they stood a good chance of being killed within a few weeks anyhow. They did not want to die virgins.

– Robert Graves, *Goodbye to All That*, 1929

For sailors, amusements ashore in the north of Scotland, in the Orkney Islands, were not abundantly available.

The British Army in France had a better deal.

Kitchener had warned his novice recruits "to keep constantly on your guard against any excesses. In this new experience you may find temptations in wine and women. You must entirely resist both".

He obviously thoroughly disapproved of a new and utterly immoral dance, the 'tango' – an early relative of the 'twerk'.

The officially sanctioned brothels, *les maisons tolérées*, and the cafés and bars behind the lines offered a blessèd escape for traumatised youth – there were lots of willing women, much in the way of wine, and a very warm welcome.

During 1915 the Royal Army Medical Corps calculated that 171,000 soldiers had visited the brothels of just one street in Le Havre.

There were well over a hundred and fifty men waiting for opening time, singing Mademoiselle from Armentières *and*

The Eighteenth Step of the Tango.

"L'union fait la force" croupions nous

Union is Strength, c.1915.

other lusty songs. Right on the dot of 6pm a red lamp over the brothel was switched on. A roar went up from the troops, accompanied by a forward lunge towards the entrance.
 — George Coppard, aged 17, *The Favourite Trench*

Under Military Law, the concealment of venereal disease, not the contraction, was a punishable crime: VD was the cause of 416,891 hospital admissions of British troops during the war – 5% of all the men enlisted.

Stoppages of pay, cruel treatments and moral castigation had no great influence. Government sensitivities, especially regarding the ultrafeminist opinions of the suffragette movement, prevented the easy availability of 'armour' – condoms. The most effective prophylactic was the Tommy's relative poverty. A British private soldier's pay was 1/- a day, a twentieth of a £1: the cheapest prostitute in France cost four days' pay.

Canadian and French troops, and latterly the American, were considerably wealthier.

It was reported that diseased girls could charge more for their services. An average hospital admission for VD was 30 days – a significant respite from the mortification and mortality of the trenches.

It must be remembered that the so-called 'Khaki Fever' was not VD, but the often desperate need of the many widowed French women who had little other financial recourse.

16

The cherry trees bend over and are shedding,
On the old road where all that passed are dead,
Their petals, strewing the grass as for a wedding
This early May morn when there is none to wed.
                    – Edward Thomas, killed aged 39, 1917

Life begins on the other side of despair.
                    – Jean-Paul Sartre, 1938

700,000 British men were killed between August 1914 and November 1918, and more than one and a half million wounded.

The upper and middle classes were particularly afflicted, a greater proportion of officers being casualties: up-front leadership and distinctive uniforms had made them all too obvious targets.

It was calculated from the 1921 National Census that there existed a surplus of 1.75 million single women: swathes of young males – husbands, fiancés, sweethearts, potential mates – had been 'buried beneath the poppies' or were in 'Davy Jones' locker'.

There were some few benefits: despite post-war redundancies, many thousands of women continued in work, and remained financially independent.

Women in a munitions factory filling shells.

A lesbian couple.

But for emotional and sexual solace women often turned to one another.

My father's half-brother, a lawyer, died aged 32, unmarried, in 1923, of chronic lung disease caused by poison gas. My father's half-sister's fiancé had been killed, and, in common with many of her contemporaries, lived to enjoy a long term same sex relationship.

17

It wasn't worth it. No war is worth it. No war is worth the loss of a couple of lives let alone thousands. T'isn't worth it ... The First World War, if you boil it down, what was it? Nothing but a family row. That's what caused it ... I would have taken the Kaiser, his son ... and the people on his side ... and bloody shot them. Out of the way and saved millions of lives. T'isn't worth it.
— Harry Patch, 'The Last Fighting Tommy', aged 100

In 1917 my father was a first year medical student and about to be 'called up' – conscripted. As a 17-year-old, I suspect that he had perceived that to volunteer as an aspirant, new fangled and perhaps glamorous pilot was preferable to being drafted into the muddy "Flanders Fields where poppies blow".

For whatever reason, he put himself forward for a commission in the newly conceived Royal Naval Air Service.

As you will understand from the speech that he gave to his colleagues and nurses in 1927, he was, almost always, a quiet and modest person – certainly not a man of mercurial temper or martial vigour – as he might have put it, 'a steady hand'.

He was the only child of an elderly second marriage: his mother had retired to a wheelchair after his birth.

He was lucky to have independent means, enough to have some small control over his future. Born into a strict Victorian

Methodist household, he was able to escape into the free-as-air venture of war.

Having had the astonishingly good fortune to have survived, he returned to his medical career, a much wiser and tougher young person – equipped with the ability to make his own mark on an optimistic new world.

A stormy on-off relationship with a glamorous divorcée eventually ended in the relative comfort of marriage.

Before my father died, I persuaded him to organise his teen-age photographs – thumb-nail contact prints – taken with his parents' gift of the new Kodak 'vest pocket' camera.

The camera was shared between friends, and many 'snaps' captured – not always happy.

Without his annotations, we would not know what these snaps had recorded.

He had photographed, week by week, his training as a pilot and his service with the Grand Fleet through to the surrender of the German High Seas Fleet – a period of just 18 months.

*   *   *

After my father's death, I found many original negatives in the bottom of his black japanned tin tube of a sea chest. They were perfectly preserved, albeit a little scratched, blurred and blotched – as you would expect from the earliest flexible roll film.

I have chosen to have these negatives enlarged by a master printer, without digital manipulation, toning or retouching.

Along with the negatives was a hurried draft of a speech given to his medical colleagues in 1927 recounting his short but traumatic military experiences.

Together, his insouciant memories and snaps are a compelling evocation of an innocent teenager's perspective on 'the war to end all wars'.

He always remained reluctant to talk about his experiences.

'High Flight'

Oh! I have slipped the surly bonds of Earth
And danced the skies on laughter-silvered wings;
Sunward I've climbed, and joined the tumbling mirth
Of sun-split clouds, – and done a hundred things
You have not dreamed of – wheeled and soared and swung
High in the sunlit silence. Hov'ring there,
I've chased the shouting wind along, and flung
My eager craft through footless halls of air...
Up, up the long, delirious, burning blue
I've topped the wind-swept heights with easy grace.
Where never lark, or even eagle flew –
And, while with silent, lifting mind I've trod
The high untrespassed sanctity of space,
* – Put out my hand, and touched the face of God.*

– John Gillespie Magee Jr, killed aged 19, 1941

Speech given by Hugh Mortimer Petty
to his hospital colleagues, 1927

Mr President   1927
Ladies & Gentlemen

I must apologise for this paper, and, if the secretary will permit me, I give my excuse that the length of time I've had to prepare it has been rather short, and therefore probably the paper will appear rather scrappy and disjointed – however here it is as composed.

    During the past ten years or so it has been my good fortune to hold a commission in the Royal Navy – first as a Flight Sub Lieut. in the Royal Naval Air Service – a Service which was merged with the Royal Flying Corps to form the Royal Air Force in April 1918 – for better or worse is a matter of opinion – mine is the latter – worse – however we cannot argue about political and national problems at this time – it's too early – the pubs aren't open yet!

S. 1516.   (Established Feb., 1916.)

ROYAL NAVAL AIR SERVICE.

PILOT'S FLYING

LOG BOOK.

Name   H.M.P$_{\text{ETTY}}$

Rank   F$_{\text{LT}}$ S$_{\text{UB}}$ L$_{\text{IEUT}}$

2,500 Bks.   4/17.—J. D. & Co., Ltd.

Basic Training at Crystal Palace, Sydenham,
8th July to 14th September 1917

Probationary Flight Officer at
RNAS Flying School Eastchurch, Isle of Sheppey

September 29th 1917 at 6.45am
First Flight
In Maurice Farman MF7 'Longhorn'.
Time in air 66 minutes, height 1,200'.
Not much good at landing.

October 10th 1917 at 7.15am
First solo
Felt quite confident.

October 19th 1917
Engine failure
So made forced landing in stubble field …
probable cause of trouble water in petrol.

November 1st 1917
First flight in Avro 504K

November 23rd 1917
Two emergency landings due to mechanical failures.

Crystal Palace

I joined the Service on July 8 1917 at the Crystal Palace – at the precise hour of 4 pm. It was a Sunday, I well remember appearing at Victoria Station wearing His Majesty's uniform for the first time, feeling extremely uncomfortable, but greatly relieved to find a good many other people also feeling uncomfortable too. We didn't wear baggy trousers either. Baggy trousers are worn so that when swabbing the decks they can be turned up over the knee – as a matter of fact that isn't done nowadays because sea boots are issued as a rule.

The Crystal Palace at this time was a Royal Naval Depot – there were I should think about 5 or 6,000 men there billeted in the Palace, and out of the Palace in the various buildings in the grounds – even training there was pretty strenuous and severe, mostly drill and physical training and a few lectures. Here I landed for a dose of Isolation as a carrier of Epidemic Cerebro Spinal Meningitis – this was rather a bore – at this time. Apparently some bright individual or individuals at Whitehall got the "wind up" about this disease. The Crystal Palace, being an excellent greenhouse, grew these cocci in large numbers, and there was an odd case I believe died – so that every officer and rating had his nasopharynx swabbed at Greenwich and a culture made. If it was positive he was immediately put into isolation for about 3 weeks.

HMS *Crystal Palace.*

Flying School

From the Crystal Palace one was drafted to a Flying School where one commenced a giddy existence – trying to break ones neck – I know better now – I did my best to go up and come down gently. The moment of one's career comes when the instructor, as he did to me one bright morning about 6am after doing about a 1/4 hour flip (we call it a flip), hops out of the machine (it was on the ground of course) in the middle of the aerodrome and says, "Now off of you go". Your heart sort of stops and you say to yourself, "Well my lad, you're for it now, it's either heaven or – … the earth!" You open your throttle, and, before you know what has happened, you're off the ground – you know that because you feel as if you were sitting on a feather bed – there is no bump bump as the machine dashes over the ground. You don't always feel, mind you, as if you were on a feather bed. There are such things as air pockets which are mighty uncomfortable if you fall into one – to drop say 100 ft to stop with a jerk gives you a bit of a jolt. However, to continue – the next thing is to turn – so you think – for a long time. When you push the dash rudder so, and you pull the joy stick over so – and there you are facing the other way – you probably feel that you're glad that you didn't have more than one cup of cocoa before you started. You know what it feels like to skid – well you do skid – for some time. However, feeling quite bucked with life, you do a few more turns, and then think it's about time you landed. Now you think hard as to how to get on to mother earth as gently as possible – so you shut your engine off and glide down. The earth gets nearer and nearer – things like and hills and buildings like dolls' houses become bigger and bigger until you realize that you are travelling like …… anything over the ground – so you get nearer and nearer until the ground seems so close that you promptly pull back the joy stick and sit down with a bump, as it were, on the ground. Well we've been up and come down again and nothing broken – and so you go on …

HMP outside his tent.

Pile of pilots.

Maurice Farman 'Longhorn'.

HMP in Cockpit of 'Longhorn'.

HMP's instructor, Flight Lieutenant Woolley.

Group of Students.

Group of Instructors.

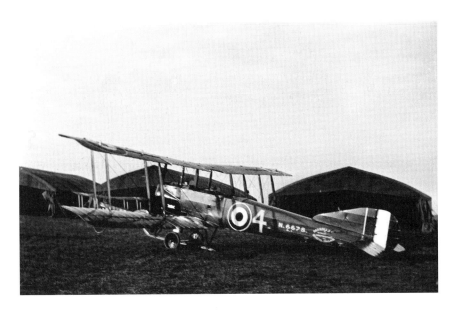

Avro 504K.

HMP in cockpit of Avro.

HMP and friends on roof of canvas Bessonneau hangar.

HMP in his new 'Arctic style' flying suit.

HMP in front of his Avro having received his 'wings'.

December 8th 1917
Transferred to RN Air Station Cranwell, Lincolnshire
[now RAF College Cranwell]

January 2nd 1918
First flight in Bristol Scout

January 14th 1918
First flight in Sopwith Pup

January 17th 1918
Forced landing in Sopwith Pup

January 20th to 22nd 1918
Graduation examination at Cranwell. Promoted to Flight
Sub-Lieutenant.
Total time to graduation, dual 6hrs 15mins, solo 36hrs 30mins.

Cranwell

Going to Cranwell, which was then the H.Q. of the R.N.A.S., and now is the H.Q. of the R.A.F., one learns to fly different types of machines. We flew BE2C's, BE2E's, Bristol Bullets, Sopwith Pups and Camels. Lectures were attended galore here in all sorts of subjects – Air Navigation, Theory of Flight, Engineering, Gunnery, Signalling. After about 2 months one had to take an examination to get one's qualifying certificate.

It was quite a stiff exam – about a dozen different papers and practicals. One then waited for the results which usually came out the same evening. Most people usually qualified, so next morning you turned up to breakfast complete with one golden stripe round the sleeve – truly one of the most important people!

At Cranwell.

The quarter deck.

Bristol Scout.

Petch survived, another medical student.

January 22nd 1918
Transferred to RN Air Station Freiston Shores, Lincolnshire
for gunnery course [later RAF School of Aerial Fighting and
Bomb Dropping]

February 22nd 1918
Transferred to RN Air Station East Fortune, near Edinburgh.
Training school for deck flying.

February 27th 1918
First flight in Sopwith 1 ½ Strutter

March 18th 1918
First flight in Sopwith Camel.
Difficulty on right hand turns – maximum height 9,000'.

March 21st 1918
Spun 2,500' from 8,500' in Camel.
Transferred to Fleet Pool, Turnhouse, Edinburgh.

Gunnery and Sea Knowledge

From Cranwell we went out to Freiston, a small place on the shores of the Wash, where we learnt more about gunnery – machine guns. A fortnight was our usual sojourn there. After the results of the exam came out, one was usually detailed for particular work. Some people were heavy handed and were given two seaters or heavy machines to fly. Others being light – shall we say "fingered" – were posted to Scout Squadrons, *ie* single seaters – they were usually the most irresponsible people. Some were sent to Seaplane Squadrons, and there were a few sent to the Grand Fleet for what was known as Deck Flying. It was to this work that I was detailed, and which put me into actual service with the Grand Fleet. We were detailed to report at East Fortune near Edinburgh, an airship station as well as a haven for aeroplanes. Here we stayed for some time – flying over the Firth of Forth – getting our sea knowledge, and learning about the silhouettes of the ships of the Grand Fleet and the Enemy so that should we spot these vessels, we could report that we had sighted a ship of such and such class.

Lewis Gun tutor.

Firth of Forth.

Sopwith 1 ½ Strutter.

Sopwith Camel.

March 26th 1918
Transferred to HMS *Nairana*, converted merchantman and
seaplane carrier used for training.

March 27th 1918
First 'take off' off from long deck of HMS *Nairana* successful
attempt. Flying 'Folder' Pup.

April 5th 1918
Transferred to RAF Station Turnhouse, Edinburgh.

April 14th 1918
Transferred to 3rd Light Cruiser Squadron, HMS *Chatham*.

May 8th 1918
First flight off HMS Chatham to Royal Naval [now RAF]
Air Station Donibristle, 2.7 miles east of Rosyth, Fife.

May 28th 1918
Transferred to RAF Turnhouse

June 1st 1918
Transferred to HMS *Caroline*
[now part of the National Historic Fleet, moored in Belfast]

Deck Flying

A further move brought us to Turnhouse which is situated about 6 miles from the south end of the Forth Bridge and about five miles north of Edinburgh. This aerodrome was called the Fleet Air Base, and from here we were drafted to ships. My first ship was the Aircraft Carrier H.M.S. *Nairana* – she was a ship from the New Zealand Frozen Meat Service, I think, and was converted into an aircraft carrier. We were sent to this ship in order to practise taking off the deck. This business was rather complicated. The machine was put on the deck so that the tail was lifted up, and the machine was in position as in flight – the tail skid had a small knob on the end: this fitted into a long piece of tubing placed in a stand. The machine was tethered as it were to the deck by a wire rope, and a special release gear fitted so that by means of another line – one jerk released the machine. The engine was put at full speed, and, on the signal from the pilot, the machine was released, and shot into the air. Whilst this was being done the ship was manoeuvred so that it was steaming directly into the wind – and therefore when the machine was released, the pull of the tractor propeller and the resistance of the wind gave the machine a chance to "rise" straight into the air.

Landing the machine was a problem which had not been thought out then – so that we had to fly ashore. Nowadays, or rather towards the very end of the war, several ships were built with flat decks so that machines could land on them with special devices for pulling them up on the deck. However, as long as we managed to get off the deck that was all that mattered. If we were at sea we had orders to land near the nearest destroyer or fly to land, which was most unlikely, or if well out over the North Sea, to make for Denmark – for this purpose we carried £20 in gold coinage for any expenses, *etc* – later we carried Danish currency. A little colony of our pilots was established thus in Denmark. The Danes interned people who actually landed on their shores, but if the machine was ditched near the shore and the pilot swam, waded or managed to get ashore in any other manner, he was sent back again. Many of the fellows refused to give their parole and amused themselves by escaping and trying to get back – quite a number succeeded too.

3rd Light Cruiser Squadron, Firth of Forth

After completing a number of practice flights in the *Nairana* we were sent back again to the shore base and then drafted to ships in the Fleet. I was sent to H.M.S. *Chatham*, a light cruiser attached to the 3rd Light Cruiser Squadron. This was my first taste of the Navy in wartime. I was greatly thrilled to be attached to the Grand Fleet – the fleet of which nobody seemed to know very much except that it inhabited the North Sea. It was truly a marvellous sight to fly above the Forth and see the lines upon lines of the great ships comprising the Fleet.

Taking off from long deck of HMS *Nairana*.

HMS *Argus*, the first 'Flat Top'.

C-class light cruiser.

Flag Captain Hallett of HMS *Chatham*, Vice Admiral Sir
Theodore, later beachmaster of Dunkirk evacuation.

HMP on turret of HMS *Caroline* with his riggers.

Sopwith Folder Pup on turret from bridge.

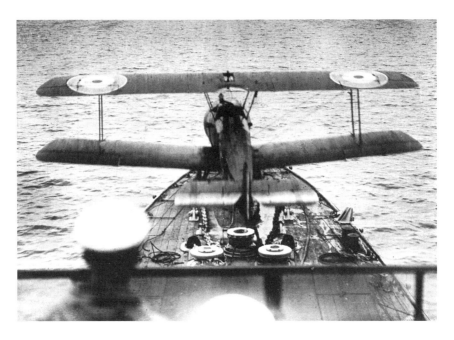

Taking off from turret.

HMS *Lion*, Flagship of battlecruiser fleet at Firth of Forth
from the air.

July 27th 1918
Transferred to HMS *Inflexible*

August 10th 1918
Spotting for ships firing. Flight off turret. Forced landing in water 7 miles east of North Berwick [a seaside town 25 miles north of Edinburgh]

From mid-September to late October 1918
Deck flying from HMS *Inflexible*, based now in Scapa Flow, Orkney Islands.

October 26th 1918
Last flight to Smoogro Air Station

HMS *Inflexible*, battlecruiser.

HMS *Inflexible* from forrard.

HMS *Inflexible*

Perhaps some of you no doubt saw the recent film *The Battles of Coronel and Falkland Islands* – those were some of the ships. I was attached to one of the actual ships which had taken part in that battle – H.M.S. *Inflexible*. I've often wondered what people thought – people living round about the Forth who looked down upon this vast fleet, lying, I might say lazily at anchor, a faint wisp of smoke coming from their funnels – looking as if they had been there for years and likely to stay there. These people would retire to bed one night and awake next morning and look down upon the Forth and rub their eyes vigorously – why? The place was absolutely deserted, not a ship to be seen – they wondered. Perhaps a few days later they would awake one morning and rub their eyes again because there before them lay the ships in exactly the same position, lazily lying at anchor, a wisp of smoke from the funnels, just as if nothing ever had happened. It must have been strange! One retired to rest at night and next morning would awake to find yourself in the middle of the North Sea, ploughing your way through those grey waters.

Convoy

Sea time varied with the ship to which you were attached – perhaps your job (of the squadron to which you were attached) was to escort food ships for Norway. You would go over to Norway north of Bergen, and take perhaps about 30 ships with you – merchant ships, mostly about 2,000 tons, and bring back another convoy perhaps the same number. It was a weary job – these ships could only steam about 10 knots at the most, whilst you would be steaming about 22 knots – so your Squadron had to steam round and round – here and there sort of go there and back to see how far it was! We always had four destroyers and about five armed trawlers. These trawlers acted like sheep dogs – they would find one straggler, so they would go round and sort of round it up.

The German submarines were of course busy during these efforts. I distinctly recall one glorious spring day – we were bringing some ships back from Norway – the sea was like a mill pond, and everybody except those on duty were lazing around – the convoy was dotted on the sea astern. I was on the bridge discussing some topic or other with the Captain on the bridge – when suddenly there was an ominous boom – I looked around and saw a sheet of flame appear amid ship of one of the convoy, smoke and the ship had gone – another boom and another ship had gone – two fair and square hits with torpedoes. Of course great excitement, action stations, full steam ahead – zigzagging hard. No ship ever steamed on a definite course – every quarter of an hour there was a change of direction – so that no lurking submarine could get a sure aim on a ship. Depth charges were dropped – I don't think we ever dropped any near the submarine. However, we went home minus two of the convoy.

Mines were often seen and duly dealt with. The wonder to me is we didn't hit more mines and get blown up – really very few ships succumbed to mines and torpedoes considering the state of the seas.

Sweeps, Coaling and Mines

Every so often the Grand Fleet used to raise steam and go to sea looking for trouble – but it never found much – the German High Sea Fleet took great care not to meet the Grand Fleet with its teeth set.

One of the worst jobs was coaling. Nowadays all the ships are oil fuelled – but in these days there were many who were coal fuel ships. It did not matter how long you had been out at sea – four, five, six days – as soon as you entered harbor, the first thing we had to do was to coal ship – and I can tell you it was no joke. After having been at sea, with rough weather, you didn't sleep much – always on the alert, never knowing when you might land in Davy Jones locker or blown sky high – to set to work and take in 1,500 tons of coal. Coaling was done at the rate of about 300 tons an hour. Every officer and man on the ship from the Commander downwards had to assist in coaling ship – all the oldest wearing apparel was brought out and by the time one had finished everybody looked like a coal miner just from the pit – everybody and everything as black as ....

– black eyelashes were the order of the day for a few days. Talking about mines – these were invented during the war. Devices called pavaranes or PV's – no, not that! – to protect ships from mines – these were two objects looking like torpedoes which were attached by lines to the bow of the vessel and towed along. By means of fins they travelled at a certain depth from the surface of the water – another line was attached to the keel of the ship at the bows – this line therefore would foul the anchorage of any mine, thrust it aside until it came to an automatic pair of jaws which closed and cut the cable of the mine and it was pushed aside, set adrift – probably sinking straight away. Every ship had a pair of these pavaranes – every merchant vessel too – and they undoubtedly saved many a ship from destruction.

Spotting

One of the main parts of the work when flying at sea was for gunnery purposes – "spotting" as it was called. Gunnery in naval warfare needs more accuracy than in land warfare – a shell dropped within say 20 yards of an object on land does a fair amount of damage – but a shell dropped within 5 yards of a ship does none at all – it goes straight to the bottom. Direct hits are the aim and object of every gunnery officer. Two lines of ships steaming along firing at each other – say 15,000 yards - 8 miles – it is not at all easy to tell when the opposing fleet has changed its course. That was our job, to signal at once when the enemy fleet changed its course so that fresh ranges could be adjusted. I well remember once in the Pentland Firth, near

Grand Fleet on a sweep.

HMP taking off.

Broadside from battleship.

Fall of shot near target.

Whaler coming alongside with HMP. HMP "made forced landing in water 7 miles west of North Berwick". He and his observer were lucky to survive, being spotted and rescued by a destroyer from the Grand Fleet.

Date and Hour.	Wind Direction and Velocity	Machine Type and No.	Passenger	Time in Air	Height
1 - 8 - 18 2·30 - 3·10.	E.	A5977 1½ Strutter	Obs Capt. Walwin	40 min	800 ft
2 - 8 - 18 3·30 - 5·20	½ ENE	6980 1½ Strutter	Obs Capt Walwin	1hr 50 min	2900 ft
10 ·8·18 9·20 - 11·20	W.	A6011 1½ Strutter	Obs Capt Walwin	2 hrs	1800.
14 · 8 · 16. 4·10 - 4·40.	W.	A5977 1½ Strutter	Obs Capt Walwin	30 min	1000
15 · 8 - 18. 10·40 - 12·20	SW	A.8224 1½ Strutter	Obs Capt Walwin	1hr 40 min	2000
20 - 8 -18	SW.	A5977 1½ Strutter	Obs Capt Walwin	35 min	1000.
21. 8·18	SW	A5977 1½ Strutter	Sub Lieut Prentice RN.	30 min	700 ft

Course	Remarks
Donibristle to Forth.	Wireless test & practice — unreliable ...
3 mls of Forth - S. incl... to. Donibristle	Spotting for ships firing — light off turret
Full of forth.	Spotting for ships firing light off turret — forced landing in water 7 miles W of N. Berwick
Donibristle	wireless practice flight.
3 mls of Forth — Donibristle	light off turret. Wireless practice no spotting due to adverse weather conditions
17 – 8 – 18 Total flying in Inflexible = 6 hrs. 40 mins	
Total flying time — 84 hrs. 38 mins	
Donibristle	wireless practice flight Very bad weather conditions
Donibristle	Test flight. weather thick

Sopwith 1 ½ Strutter coming in.

Coming alongside 1.

Coming alongside 2.

Having hook attached.

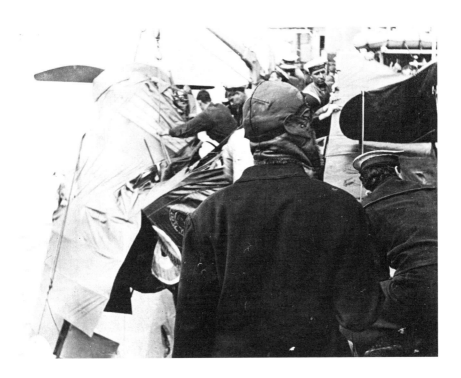

Coming on board – HMP in foreground.

New Sopwith 1 ½ Strutter coming on board.

Sopwith 1 ½ Strutter blown off its turret in North Sea gale.

HMS *Tiger*, battlecruiser.

At ease on HMS *Tiger*.

HMS *Tiger* from aft.

Scapa Flow, flying above and between the target and the ships, getting somewhere in the vicinity of the trajectory of the shells – 12" too. I couldn't understand why the weather had suddenly become so bad – until I was suddenly aware of a good crack on the back of the head from my observer with a spanner. I turned around and saw him waving and gesticulating – you cannot hear a word for the noise of your engine. I knew what adjectives he was using all right, and I suddenly realised as a low whistle heard, mind you, above the roar of the engine and a terrific rocking of the machine that I was wandering about and much too near to be comfortable to 12 inch shells weighing half a ton or more flying through the air. Needless to say I got out of the way very quick.

Armistice and Surrender

One of the most interesting - and one of the most amazing, believe me absolutely amazing, sights was the surrender of the German High Sea Fleet. I was fortunate enough to be present on that memorable day. After the negotiations which had taken place with the German delegates on board the *Queen Elizabeth* – flagship of the Grand Fleet – the rendezvous was arranged. The day before I remember we had an inspection by the King of the Grand Fleet, and the same evening – it was the great topic of the Fleet – "Would they turn up?" Nobody thought that it was possible. We just couldn't see how the German Fleet, which we had hardly ever set eyes upon, could just walk in and say – "Here we are". Arguments went on until late into the night. We were due to sail at 4am so everybody retired still wondering. I awoke up to find myself at sea once again – the morning was fine but very misty. On deck one looked around and saw long lines fading into the mist of ships ploughing their way through the waves of the North Sea. 9am was the appointed time for the rendezvous – all the guns were loaded but not trained out, there were no risks taken! Everybody who was above decks – there are not a large number of people above decks when a ship is in action - paced up and down. "Would they turn up?" was the question asked by everybody. 9am approached and on the hour being struck on and the ship's bell – everybody looked ahead and tried to pierce that mist – the tension was extreme. We knew that our leading ship, which was H.M.S. *Cardiff*, should have met the leading ship of the German High Sea Fleet. 9.30am – there was a stir – the word was passed from the look-out at the mast head – the *Cardiff*! – the word *Cardiff* went round to every man, and then behind steaming silently – loomed up the German Battle Cruiser S.M.S. *Seydlitz*. "They've surrendered!!" went the cry – and so all those who were on deck gazed upon the scene with feelings of relief – and also with a feeling of satisfaction. One after another ships of the German fleet appeared – they were named by everyone as each appeared – ships never seen by the majority of people, ships recognized by their silhouettes which we had learned – but they came one by one! Believe me a truly amazing sight! – then followed cruisers, light cruisers – and destroyers – we had collected about 130 destroyers I believe, and these ships escorted about 70 odd German destroyers – add them up, 210 odd! – all of them in an array such as will never be seen again. The sea was literally black with ships.

By about 2pm the last German ship had passed and the

HMS *Hood*, 43,000 tons, sunk by *Bismarck* on 24th May 1941 with
the loss of 1,415 of the crew of 1,418.

HMS *Furious*, aircraft carrier, in dazzle camouflage developed by
the 'Vorticist' artists at the Royal Academy.

HMS *Furious* and HMS *Glorious* in the Firth of Forth – Armistice Day, 11th November 1918.

Officers on HMS *Inflexible*, 11th November.

Review of the Grand Fleet, King George V on board
HMS *Oak*, 20th November.

Beatty saluting on board flagship HMS *Queen Elizabeth*,
20th November.

Beatty on his bridge.

Grand Fleet sailing to accept surrender of German High Seas Fleet,
22nd November, early morning.

HMS *Indomitable*, sister ship of HMS *Inflexible* at surrender.

SMS *Seydlitz*, battlecruiser, survivor of Jutland, first German ship to surrender.

German light cruiser at surrender 1.

German Light cruiser at surrender 2.

Squadron I was in was the sort of rearguard – we about turned and came in last. Such was the end of the High Sea Fleet of Germany.

They were formed up into a square in the Forth guarded by 2 Battle Squadrons and 2 Battle Cruiser Squadrons – my Squadron, a Battle Cruiser one, was the last one to complete the square of guard ships, and we had to steam around three sides of the square to take up our appointed billet. Passing across the bows of one of the German light cruisers – as many men from down below were allowed to come on deck – and in the silence of that memorable day – our crew gazed in dead silence on the crew of this enemy ship – neither crew had seen each other's ship before. Red armlets denoting the workers representatives were quite evident with considerable numbers among the crews of the German ships.

Having taken our stations up – each ship had so many officers and men detailed to go over to the surrendered ships to search them. I was not able to wangle a trip unfortunately but I heard the accounts from the other officers. The Captain of the surrendered ships met our officers and escorted them to his cabin where the necessary papers were signed and handed over – and a tour of the ship began. The guns had no breech blocks – there were no range finders – articles of which we were very anxious to get hold. The magazines were full of potatoes and the shell rooms stank badly of onions! The ships were anything but clean – apparently all orders of the Captain were handed through these fellows with red armlets.

At sunset the German flags were hauled down and a very famous signal of Beatty's was sent – stating that the German Flag will be hauled down at sunset and will not again be hoisted – a truly bitter blow for them! I have a copy of the original signal sent to the ship to which I was attached. I haven't got it here unfortunately. That episode more or less ended my dealings with the Grand Fleet which was shortly afterwards broken up into various Squadrons detailed for foreign stations.

November 24th 1918
Transferred to HMS *Marlborough*

HMS *Marlborough* Sunday Parade at Scapa Flow.

Going ashore at Scapa Flow.

And when they ask us how dangerous it was,
We never will tell them, we never will tell them –
How we fought in some café,
With wild women night and day –
'Twas the wonderfullest war you ever knew.
And when they ask us, and they're certainly going to ask us,
Why on our chests we do not wear the Croix de Guerre,
We never will tell them,
We never will tell them…..

– Cole Porter, 'War Song', 1918

HMP on his motorcycle.

HMP newly qualified with his first car.

My mother to be.

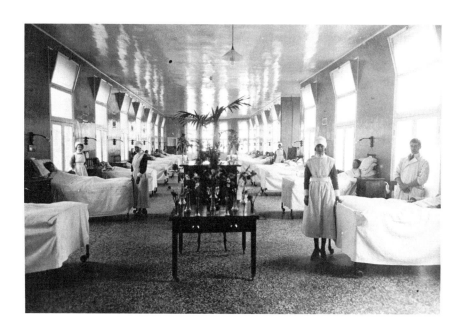

HMP in hospital ward.

HMP with operating theatre staff.

182

'Past Days are Hieroglyphs'

Past days are hieroglyphs
Scrawled behind the brows
Scarred deep with iron blows,
Upon the thundered tree
Of memory.

Marvellous mad beliefs
(To believe that you believed!),
Plain and time-unthieved,
Scratched and scrawled on the tree
Of memory.

Time, good graver of griefs,
Those words sapped with my soul,
That I read as of old and whole,
What eye in the world shall see
On this covered tree?

1915

– Isaac Rosenberg, killed in action 1st April 1918

List of Illustrations

Unless listed otherwise below, the images reproduced in this book were taken by Hugh Mortimer Petty.

Chapter 1

Chapter 2

Field Marshal Horation Herbert Kitchener, The Art Archive/
    Imperial war Museum/Eileen Tweedy (p. 13).
Boy (1st class) John Travers Cornwell, The Art Archive/Eileen
    Tweedy (p. 14).

Chapter 3

Admiral of the Fleet John Arbuthnot 'Jacky' Fisher, Library of
    Congress (p. 18).
Grand Admiral Alfred von Tirpitz, Library of Congress (p. 19).
'U-boats', Library of Congress (p. 20).

Chapter 4

Scapa Flow by Sir John Lavery (1917), The Art Archive/DeA
    Picture Library/G. Nimatallah (p. 23).
The British Grand Fleet at anchor in the Firth of Forth, The
    Art Archive/Imperial War Museum (p. 23).
The North Sea, unattributed (p. 24).
Sir James Alfred Ewing, Topfoto (p. 26).

Chapter 5

Guglielmo Marconi, The Art Archive/DeA Picture Library/A.
    De Gregorio (p. 30).

Chapter 6

'England expects every man to do his duty', The Art Archive/
    DeA Picture Library (p. 34).
Training ship *Mercury*, Topfoto (p. 35).

Chapter 7

Chapter 8

Chapter 9

Chapter 10

Chapter 11

Chapter 12

Chapter 13

Chapter 14

Chapter 15

Chapter 16

The Speech